Steamed and Steamy

Recipes from the Steampunk World of Industralia

A Novel Cookbook

Written by Lori Alden Holuta

Cover Design by Tanya Paterson

Edited by Ken Holuta

Author's cover photo courtesy of
John-Michael O'Brien at PhotoNinjas.net

Disclaimer

Cooking and baking involves inherent danger. Sharp tools and high heat are often a part of the preparation process. You may be allergic to certain foods. The author has no way of knowing your skill level or dietary restrictions. So it is up to you, gentle reader, to exercise discretion and common sense before preparing these recipes. The author is not responsible for any accidents or personal harm resulting from the preparation of food using the recipes and instructions in this book. These recipes are to be used at your own risk.

Graphic Credits

Vintage graphics used throughout this cookbook are in the public domain. Many of them have been spruced up by The Graphics Fairy.

**Dedicated To
The Foodies Who Inspire Me**

Joyce Wagner, Ann Wagner, Art Wagner, Vaneta Wagner, Michelle Adams, Jane Miller, Aunt Marlene, Delores Jensen, Carol Touchette, Kara Roff-Jensen, Kronda Seibert, Christine Bamberger, Nikki Frazier, Laura Byno, Cathy Karas, Lynne Lavender, and nearly everyone on Plurk.

**In Memory Of Those
Who Taught Me Well**

Great-Gramma Brown
Gramma Levely
Virginia Holuta

If you're craving Victorian era trivia, steampunk news, fun (and free!) activities for kids of all ages, and access to the mind of author Lori Alden Holuta, then "Postcards From Industralia" should be dropping into your mail box once a month. Subscribe here:

brassbrightcity.com/newsletter

Table of Contents

This is an overview of the recipes contained in this cookbook. The section titled "How To Use This Cookbook" should help you to… well, use this cookbook.

You will find a traditional recipe index in the back of the book.

LUNCH

DINNER

Introduction

This cookbook features foods enjoyed by the characters in my food-centric stories, set in the fictional steampunk country of Industralia. The recipes draw from dining adventures within the pages of *The Flight To Brassbright* and *The Legend of The Engineer*. I've also included recipes from my upcoming novel, *Down The Tubes*, Volume Two of the Brassbright Chronicles. You can consider those recipes a sneak peek at the novel!

I come from a long lineage of foodies. Their legacy and inspiration fills my recipe box—a converted hardwood floppy disk file box—as well as many bulging three-ring binders, and a collection of offbeat cookbooks.

But even though I've been given so many traditional family recipes, already fine-tuned to perfection by my relatives, I can't help being a 'tweaker'. What you'll find in this cookbook will be many recipes that, over time, have been adapted to my own personal style.

When I am writing and my characters get hungry, it feels natural to draw from my own favorite recipes to feed them. As their creator, I like to make sure they get plenty of good food to eat.

I am grateful for everyone who came before me, those foodies throughout the centuries who lit a fire, simmered a pot, and wondered, "Did I already salt that?"

How To Use This Cookbook

Industralia is a hardworking country, where everyone firmly believes in the value of a lavish breakfast.

Industralians may skip lunch, and even delay dinner if necessary, but they *never* skip breakfast. However, this cookbook tries to strike a balance and include all the meals.

Because I am including excerpts from the books alongside these recipes, it seems cozy to keep together all the dishes that are served as a meal. So for example, 'Dinner at The Bonnet House' is presented as an entire meal, including dessert.

Just to keep things interesting, some of the recipes are also offered in narrative form. For example, a late night breakfast at the Grand Sterling is an excerpt pulled directly from *The Flight To Brassbright*. In other words, not all recipes are written in traditional form. Some are anecdotal in nature. Cookie's circus breakfast is told in his 'rustic' narrative form. Hannah Vanbrugh's tomato soup recipe is revealed by her inner thoughts. Other recipes are grouped as best I could manage. Industralians are very difficult people to pigeonhole, and apparently so are their recipes.

Please do not panic over these complex culinary cow paths. If you are looking for a particular type of recipe, simply turn to the recipe index in the back of the book, which is organized in a traditional, logical manner.

Since I am an American, these recipes are presented using the U.S. measuring system. It is an unfortunate reality that there is no international standard for cooking and baking, so I am using the one I am most familiar with. Luckily there are conversion charts available on the internet, for those of you using a different measuring system. So remember that tablespoons and teaspoons are different amounts, and our cups are not the same as a teacup!

Finally, some important advice—always read a recipe three times before you start cooking or baking! The first time, read to appreciate the recipe and to learn if this is a dish you would enjoy preparing. The second time, read to check your available ingredients and equipment. The third time, read to understand the cooking method. Then... have yourself some kitchen fun!

Crack of Dawn Breakfast at
Winthrop & Hammerschlinger's
Travelling Emporium of Amazement

In that side of the wagon was a wide counter holding three huge coffee pots, while clouds of steam wafted out from behind them. As we screeched to a halt at the counter, a red-faced man leaned out of the steam to look at us. He was wearing a green bandana tied around his head and a red apron. The bandana failed to contain all of his glossy, curly black hair.

The apron stains could have been used as a menu—I saw egg yolks, strawberry jam, and what probably was bacon grease, all mixed together to create a design the original seamstress never could have imagined. ~ From *The Flight To Brassbright*

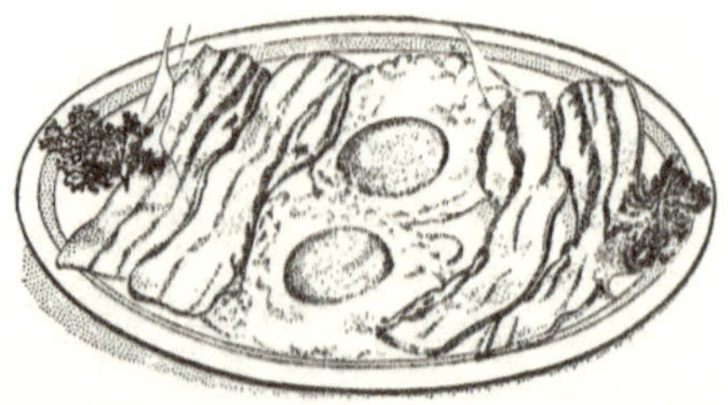

Cookie is not the sort to write down his recipes on cards and keep them in a box. He learned to cook at his uncle's diner, because that's what family did—anyone tall enough to see the stovetop was put to work. Receiving the occasional swat with a wooden spoon and a hurriedly barked, "Faster, kid! Hungry mechanics don't have all day to wait while you dawdle!" inspired John Coogan, nicknamed 'Cookie', to learn how to make food in a hurry.

His culinary motto is "More grease! Food can't be fast if it's not lubricated!" His recipes will be transcribed in his own words. Do not look for precise measurements, as Cookie doesn't use measuring equipment.

Fried Eggs for a Multitude

Cookie says, "My secret for perfect sunny side up eggs is oil. A lot of oil. Grab a 14 inch skillet and pour a bunch of glugs of oil into it. You want it about an inch deep. Turn up the heat to medium high, and get that oil hot enough to almost smoke, but not so hot you'll burn your wagon down.

"If you can, crack four eggs at once. That's a skill you'll need to practice, but it's mighty impressive once you got it. Crack 'em right into the oil, and try to keep them as far apart as you keep your in-laws at the holidays.

"You'll know you have the right amount of oil if the egg whites are drowning, while the yolks are riding high in the open air. Just as soon as the whites are set, lift the eggs out with a slotted spoon. Dangle them over the pan a few seconds to let most of the oil drain off, then get them onto plates quick like. Then grab four more eggs and keep going. Top off the oil whenever you see the dipstick running low. Don't stop drowning eggs 'til everyone's had their fill.

"As for toppings, you got your salt, you got your pepper. You don't need anything else. If I catch you puttin' cheese on your eggs you're going to get a lecture."

Bombastic Baked Bacon

After wiping a copious amount of grease off of his hands, Cookie shares what he thinks is the best way ever to bring home the bacon.

"My oven's almost always filled up with loaves of bread, but every morning I make room to squeeze in a couple of large pans of bacon. Find your biggest baking pans and line them with some foil. Lay out all your bacon slices on the foil and bake them for 15-20 minutes in a 400 degree Fahrenheit oven. No need to turn 'em, you don't have time for that, and both sides will cook just fine thanks to the foil. Throw some absorbent paper on a large platter, and use a pair of tongs—not your fingers unless you don't like them much—to lift the cooked bacon onto the platter."

Cookie's Sideshow Bread

Cookie slathered a thick slice of bread with enough butter to grease a wagon wheel, folded it in half and downed it in two bites. Then he leaned back and slurped a cup of hot coffee as he talked.

"The reason I bake a lot of bread every day is so the circus folk can have their toast with butter and jam every morning, and still have enough left for making sandwiches late at night. You got any idea how much bread a circus can eat in a day? Whatever you guessed, triple it.

"What I do is make a plain, wholesome sourdough bread. I tear off a chunk of my starter from inside its crock, which I keep safe in a back corner of the cook wagon. Mix that with five fistfuls of flour and two hand-scoops of water, then pinch in some salt and be generous. I wrestle all that together and let it rest under a fairly clean towel. Once it rises up, I punch it down and it takes a nap. When it wakes up, I punch it down again. Reminds me a lot of my childhood with my older brothers, now that I think on it. One more rise, and then it goes in the oven till it's golden brown and has a good echo when I knock on it.

"Since I work from memory and use these big old hands as measuring cups, I'd be here all day trying to work out measurements for you, since I can see right now your hands are a lot smaller than my old meat hooks.

"Just remember, don't bother making it too fancy and stay away from heavy breads. That's important! You got to find a balance between keeping everyone fed, but not making them fall over all food stupid before they get their work done."

Shirley's Strangely Simple Strawberry Jam

Cookie doesn't make everything himself, he has his sources for special treats. For example, he tells us, "I know a woman named Shirley, who's got the most fantastic strawberry fields. And I like that she sells her jam in great big crocks, so I don't have to fuss around with tiny jam jars. I'm feeding a circus, not hosting a tea party, after all. Last year she told me her secret fruit jam recipe, and it's dead simple, it is. When I asked her how much pectin she used, she gave me such a glare."

"Pectin? I don't need no stinking pectin!" she bragged. I got to admit that Shirley's one heck of a strong-willed woman, and maybe her jam is just so intimidated by her that it can't help but gel."

Ingredients
2 cups white granulated sugar
3 tablespoons lemon juice (fresh if possible)
2 cups hulled and halved strawberries

Instructions
Put a small ceramic or glass plate in your freezer to chill. You'll use this later in the recipe.
Mix the sugar and lemon juice in a medium saucepan.
Simmer the mixture on very low heat for 10 minutes, or until all the sugar has dissolved.
Add the strawberries and continue to cook over very low heat.
When the strawberries release their juice and the mixture begins to slowly boil, take the small plate out of the freezer.
Use a spoon to dip a small amount of juice out of the saucepan and pour it onto the cold plate.
If the juice gels, your saucepan of jam is done. If it doesn't, keep the saucepan at a rolling boil and continue testing the juice on the plate until it does. Put the plate back in the freezer between juice tests.
When your juice gels, turn off the heat and ladle the jam into two pint canning jars.
If you know how to preserve jam, process the jars in a hot water bath for 10 minutes.
If you are not a canner, keep the jam in the refrigerator and use it up within three weeks.

Breakfast with Letitica in Steamkettle Bay

Nathaniel and Letitica were seated at the kitchen table, which had been heaped with platters of crispy-edged over-easy eggs, a tall stack of pancakes, thick slices of ham and even thicker slices of crusty brown bread.

"I stopped by the market on me way, and those eggs are so fresh, the hens are still wondering if they actually laid them!" he exclaimed.
~ From *The Flight To Brassbright*

Crispy-Edged Over-Easy Eggs

Ingredients
Olive oil or cooking fat of your choice
3 eggs
Salt and pepper

Instructions
Heat a cast iron skillet on high heat for 1 minute.
Add enough oil or fat to cover the bottom of the pan, and let it heat for 30 seconds.
Crack the eggs into the pan, turn the heat down to medium, then step back as the oil or fat will occasionally pop.
When the edges of the eggs start to brown, gently lift each egg and turn it over in the pan.
Count to five, then lift each egg carefully from the pan with a thin metal spatula. Using a thin spatula allows you to loosen any bits of egg that might be sticking to the pan.
Transfer cooked eggs to a warmed platter, but don't hold them for very long before serving.
Season with salt and pepper to taste.
Repeat the process as needed.
Do not reheat eggs or they will cease to be over easy.

Perfectly Pleasant Puffy Pancakes

Ingredients

1-1/2 cups white all-purpose flour
1 tablespoon white granulated sugar
1 teaspoon coarse salt
2-3/4 teaspoons baking powder
1 large egg, lightly beaten
1-1/4 cups milk
2 tablespoons unsalted butter, melted
Vegetable oil
Pats of butter for serving
Warm maple syrup

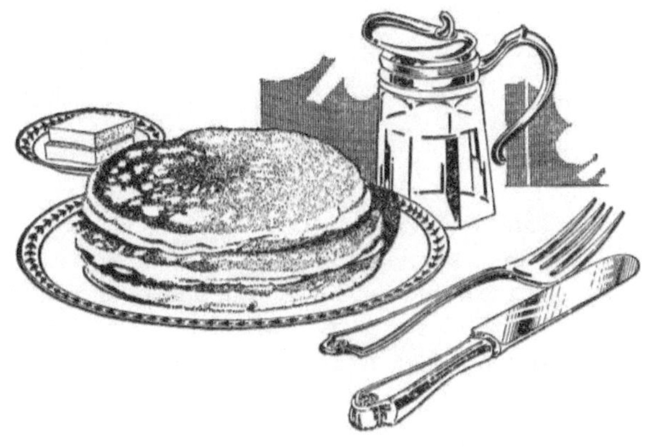

Instructions

Heat oven to 200 degrees Fahrenheit and place a heatproof platter inside.
In a large bowl, mix the flour, sugar, salt, and baking powder together
with a whisk.
Add the egg, milk, and butter to the dry mixture. Whisk gently to blend.
Let the batter rest for 10 minutes.
Heat a griddle or skillet over medium-high heat.
Add a thin coating of oil to the pan. Tilt the pan to coat it evenly.

Pour in 1/4 cup of batter for each pancake. When the pancakes start to
bubble, turn them with a spatula and cook another minute, or until the
bottom side is golden and the pancake is fully cooked. (Continued)

(Puffy Pancakes Continued)

For some mysterious reason, the first batch of pancakes will often look
flat and pale. Science has yet to explain this phenomenon. They'll taste
just fine, though.
Lift the pancakes from the pan and stack them on the warmed platter in
the oven. Keep making pancakes until the batter is gone.

Serve pancakes hot, topped with pats of butter and warm syrup. Put the
butter dish and the syrup bottle on the table, as everyone will want more.

Easy Skillet Ham

Ingredients
Country ham

Instructions
Cut the ham into 1/4 inch thick slices.
Warm a skillet over low heat.
Lay slices of ham in the skillet. Fill the pan, but do not overlap the slices.
Cover the skillet with a lid and let the ham simmer on low heat for 10
minutes.
With a fork, turn the slices over a few times during the cooking process.

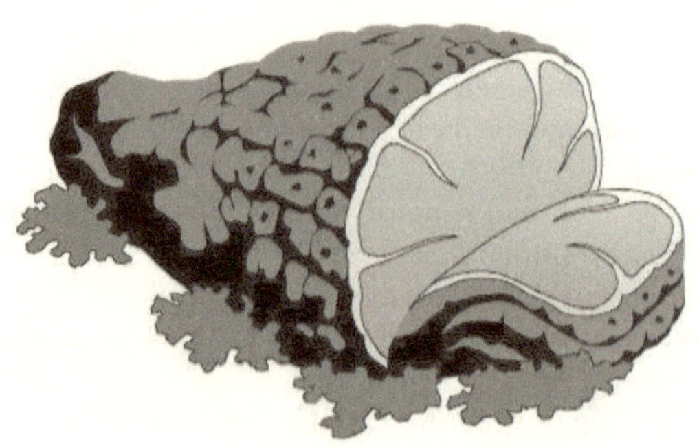

Crispity Crusty Brown Bread

Ingredients
5-1/3 cups whole wheat flour
2-1/4 teaspoons active dry yeast
1 tablespoon salt
1 tablespoon white granulated sugar or honey
2 cups lukewarm water

Instructions
"Proof" the yeast by adding it to 1/4 cup of the lukewarm water. When the water turns foamy, that's your proof that the yeast is active.
Mix all the ingredients, either with your hands, or use an electric mixer with bread hooks.
Let the dough rest for 15 minutes.
If the dough feels too wet, add a bit more flour. If it feels too dry, add a bit more water.
Knead the dough by hand on a floured surface for 10 minutes. If you are using bread hooks, 5 minutes of kneading is enough.
Place the dough into a large glass bowl (at least twice as large as your dough ball).
Cover the bowl with a clean kitchen towel.
Let the dough rise for an hour or until it doubles in size.
Punch down the puffy dough with your fist.
Shape the dough into a round or oval loaf.
Line a baking sheet with parchment paper.
Place dough on the parchment paper.
Cover the loaf again with the kitchen towel.
Let dough rise another hour.
Heat oven to 400 degrees Fahrenheit.
Remove towel and slide the baking sheet, with the parchment paper and dough still on it, into the oven.
Bake the loaf for 30 minutes or until golden brown.
When done, the loaf should sound hollow when you rap your knuckles against the crust.

Rise and Shine!
Bed and Breakfast at the Bonnet House

As predicted, my nose woke me up to announce that smoky bacon seemed to be on the menu this morning. My stomach growled a query about eggs, and my bleary eyes wondered about coffee. With all that conversation going on, I had no choice but to get up.

Soon the crew tromped down the stairs, yawning and scratching, mumbling words like 'coffee, hot, strong, now'. Lucky for them the coffee was indeed hot and strong, and I gratefully drank two large mugs. We dined on crispy bacon, fluffy scrambled eggs, fried potatoes and onions, and soft bread with butter and jam. There wasn't much conversation, as we were all busy trying to finish waking up, while stuffing our faces with Cook's delicious food.
~ From *The Flight To Brassbright*

This full breakfast should serve an airship crew of three plus one passenger, or eight hungry 'normal' diners.

Crispy Bacon for a Crew

Ingredients
12 to 20 slices of bacon, or as many slices as you can fit on your wire racks.

Instructions
Set a wire rack (such as is used for cooling cookies) on a cookie sheet with raised-sides. Depending on the size of your rack and your sheet, you may be able to fit two racks on the cookie sheet.
The cookie sheet must have raised sides, as the intent is to let the bacon fat warm up, render, and then drip away from the bacon. This recipe is for *crispy* bacon, not *greasy* bacon.
Turn on the oven, and set it to 450 degrees Fahrenheit.
Do not wait for the oven to warm up before sliding in your pan of bacon. The gradual warming of the oven will allow the bacon fat to warm gently, render, and drip onto the cookie sheet as the bacon reaches the right temperature to cook through.
Cook the bacon for 20 minutes.
Check the bacon for crispiness, and if desired, cook a bit longer.
20 minutes should do the trick for thin sliced bacon. Thick sliced bacon may require a few more minutes, but keep a sharp eye on it.
When the bacon has reached the desired crispiness, remove the pan from the oven.
Using tongs, carefully move cooked bacon onto a serving platter.
There should be no need to drain the bacon, as the wire racks have accomplished that task for you.

Take a moment to pause and admire your pristine stovetop, which is completely devoid of bacon grease splatters. Now carry the platter of bacon to your hungry breakfasters, while smiling serenely.

Cheesy as You Please,
Fluffy as a Cloud Scrambled Eggs

Ingredients

10 eggs
4 tablespoons cold water
1-1/2 teaspoons baking powder
4 tablespoons butter, room temperature
Salt and pepper
1/4 cup grated cheese of your choice
(although sharp Cheddar is *never* a bad choice)

Instructions

In a large bowl, whip the eggs, water, and baking powder with a whisk until thoroughly blended. If you are energetic and strong of arm, keep whipping until the mixture becomes a fluffy froth for even fluffier eggs. Why do we add cold water? Because we want steam! As the water turns to steam, it will help make the eggs fluffier. You can use milk instead of water for this purpose, if you wish.
Let the egg mixture sit for 5 minutes.
Put the butter into a large sauté pan over medium heat. When the butter is completely melted, pour in the egg mixture. Turn heat to medium-low. As the eggs start to cook, lift them and gently turn them over on themselves, letting them gently break into 'curds' as they set.
Dash the eggs with salt and pepper about halfway through.

Hale and Hearty Fried Potatoes and Onions

Ingredients

6 large, sturdy Russet potatoes, scrubbed and set aside to dry. Leave the peel on as it is very healthy, and tasty too.
1 tablespoon salt
3 tablespoons olive oil
3 tablespoons butter, room temperature
1/2 teaspoon Hungarian paprika
Salt and pepper for seasoning
One large sweet onion (if you can obtain a Vidalia onion, all the better)
1 tablespoon coarsely chopped fresh parsley
1 cup sour cream

Instructions

Fill a large saucepan with water, leaving room for the potatoes. Make sure the saucepan is large enough to submerge all the potatoes in the water.
Add a tablespoon of salt to the water and bring it to a boil.
When the water boils, gently place the potatoes into the saucepan and boil for 20 minutes.
Test the potatoes by sticking them with a fork. If the fork slides into the potato easily, they are done.
Empty the saucepan into a large colander to drain off the water.
Let the potatoes sit in the colander and cool down enough for you to handle them without burning your fingers.
Add the oil, butter, and paprika to a large, heavy frying pan.
Warm the pan over medium heat, stirring ingredients gently until they are melted and blended.
Do not peel the potatoes. Slice them into rounds about 1/8 inch thick.
Chop the onion into pieces no larger than 1/2 inch.
Add the sliced potatoes and diced onion to the warm frying pan.
Add salt and pepper to taste.
Cook on medium heat for 20-25 minutes. Now and then, lift and turn the potatoes to be sure all sides get a chance to brown and crisp. Use care when turning, as the potatoes can easily break.
When done, lift the potatoes onto a warm serving platter.
Scatter chopped fresh parsley over the potatoes.
Serve with a dish of sour cream on the side.

Silky Soft White Milk Bread

Ingredients
1/2 cup lukewarm water
1 packet active dry yeast (2-1/4 teaspoons)
2 teaspoons white granulated sugar
3 cups white all-purpose flour
1/3 cup white all-purpose flour (separate from the other flour)
1 egg
1 teaspoon salt
1/4 cup butter, melted
1/4 cup milk

Instructions
In a medium bowl, combine warm water, yeast, and 1 teaspoon of sugar. Stir the mixture, then let it sit for about 10 minutes. This mixture should turn foamy. If it does not, the yeast did not activate. You will need to try this step again, with fresher yeast. When you have an active, foamy mixture, proceed with the rest of this recipe.
Sift 3 cups of flour into a large bowl, then push the flour towards the bowl's sides to form a hollow center.
Pour the yeast mixture into the hollow center of the flour, along with the egg, the second teaspoon of sugar, the salt, and the melted butter.
With an electric mixer and a dough hook, or a large wooden spoon, mix the dough.
Add the milk and briefly mix again.
If the dough is very sticky, add a little of the remaining flour and keep working the dough until it forms a ball. The dough should be soft.
Grease a large glass or ceramic bowl.
Place the dough ball in the greased bowl, lay a clean kitchen towel over the top, and let it rise. This should take about an hour.
The dough should have doubled in size before going to the next step.
With your fist, punch the dough down.
Turn the dough out onto a lightly floured surface.
With your hands, shape the dough into a loaf.
Place your dough-loaf into a greased 9 inch by 5 inch bread pan.
Cover the dough with the towel and let it rise again for a half hour.
Bake at 375 degrees Fahrenheit for 30 minutes, or until golden brown.
Let the bread cool for 10 minutes before removing it from the pan.

Story Interlude
A Late Night Breakfast In
The Grand Sterling's Basement Kitchen

When I arrived at the kitchen, I was encouraged to find that it was well-lit and in use, even at this late hour. A man dressed in a fine white uniform and wearing what looked like a puffy pillow on his head was standing at the stove, frying eggs and sausage. When the swinging door creaked behind me, he looked up.

"Evening miss! No need to come all the way down here, you could have used the pneumatic message tube in your room to place your food order."

"Oh, I'm not a guest of the hotel proper. I'm staying with a friend in The Haven for a few days. I was feeling restless though, and decided to go exploring. Must have been the wonderful smell of that food you're frying that drew me in here," I said, suddenly realizing how hungry I had become. It had been a long time since my last meal, and only the excitement of the day had kept me from noticing that I hadn't eaten anything.

He smiled at my broad hint disguised as a compliment, and turned back to the stove. Flipping his sauté pan deftly, the eggs he was cooking somersaulted perfectly. "Pardon me while I finish up this order. There's a hungry businessman on the fourth floor who's waiting for these."

"You certainly do have a way with that pan, sir! I once cooked for an... um, entertainment troupe, and they had stomachs that went deeper than most wells. I know it can be hard work keeping everyone fed, but you make it look like child's play."

"Ah, another chef, are you? It's very nice to meet you. My name is Chef Jacques Jaquart, and I trained at the Fryworthy Institute of Hotel Comestibles," he said, nudging the sausage links with a spatula. "And where did you receive your culinary training, miss?" he queried, prodding me to more formally introduce myself and to reveal where I had learned to cook.

I hesitated. Cracking eggs for a circus wasn't anywhere close to formal training. Still, I'd cooked lots of wholesome food in a hot, crowded outdoor wagon, and I figured he'd at least admire the hard work involved. I smiled in what I hoped was a charming manner and said, "My name is Constance and I trained with

Winthrop & Hammerschlinger's Travelling Emporium of Amazement. Preparing meals for a large circus troupe is no small matter, and I learned a lot from rough cooking on the road."

"Well, well, well! I am impressed. A fine school can teach plenty of elegant recipes and fancy techniques, but I'm sure you could show me a few tricks that weren't in the official curriculum," he replied with a laugh, as he placed the eggs onto a gleaming white plate, sitting on a silver platter. Then he quickly scooped up a mountain of fried potatoes and placed them next to the eggs.

"Well, I could teach you how to crack two eggs at once!" I offered. I was relieved and happy to have been accepted as a fellow chef, even though each of us had learned the craft in wildly different ways.

Chef Jaquart laughed and waved a dismissing hand. "Only two eggs? Students at Fryworthy become adept at cracking four eggs before they graduate. In fact, it's part of the final exam." He lifted the sausage links from the stove to the plate, then reviewed the meal. He nodded in satisfaction, then placed a silver-plated dome over the food to keep it warm. To finish the order, he added a glass of orange juice, as well as silverware and a fine linen napkin.

"Well, the grille's available now, Constance. Why don't you show me how you cooked breakfast back at Winters and Hammerstein's Travelling Whatchamacallit?" he challenged me, handing over a fresh spatula and gesturing towards the stove.

There was no good reason to correct his amusing mispronunciation of the circus name, especially since it happily reminded me of Missus Liddle's magnificent word mutilations. I took the spatula with a determined swipe of my hand and said, "May I have four eggs please?"

Five minutes later I dished up two eggs on one plate and two on another, set slabs of buttery grilled toast on each, and scooped up a large spoonful of diced fruit to complete the meal.

"Breakfast a la Boom Boom," I said with a flourish. "I would be delighted if you'd share a meal with me, Chef."

~ From *The Flight To Brassbright*

The Hungry Duck Restaurant's
Hurry-Up Lunch

"Good afternoon, Maryanne. One sautéed flaked fish sandwich with Cheddar cheese, and some of your delicious fried potato slices with spiced tomato sauce, please," Sterling said to his favorite waitress, just as soon as he'd stepped inside the Hungry Duck.

Maryanne, wearing a cheerful yellow dress patterned with the restaurant's namesake waterfowl, smiled warmly at the familiar customer. "Sure thing Mister Summberbee! Follow me please?" She seated him at a small table near the windows. The table was set with ceramic salt and pepper shakers shaped like ducks, a fine linen napkin, gleaming silverware and a small silver stand holding a pasteboard advertisement for the day's special desserts. "Back in a flash with hot coffee," she said, then darted back to the kitchen. "Tuna melt with fries and ketchup, Trudy! And make it quick, we're on Sterling Time!"
~ From *Down The Tubes*

Sterling's Favorite Tuna Melt

Ingredients
1 can (5 ounces) light or white tuna packed in water
2 slices red onion
1 celery rib
1 teaspoon mustard
4 tablespoons mayonnaise
Salt and pepper
Garlic powder (optional)
1 finely chopped hard-boiled egg (optional)
2 slices rye bread
6 tablespoons butter, room temperature
A small block of sharp Cheddar cheese
4 bread and butter pickles (Continued)

(Tuna Melt Continued)

Instructions

Drain the water from the tuna, and discard the liquid.
Flake the tuna into a mixing bowl, using a fork to break the chunks into loose flakes.
Finely dice 2 slices of red onion and half a celery rib.
Add the diced onion and celery to the tuna.
Slice the other half of the celery rib into sticks and set aside.
Add mustard and mayonnaise to the tuna mixture.
Season the mixture with salt, pepper, and garlic powder to taste.
Blend the tuna mixture thoroughly, being sure to break up any chunks of tuna you may have missed earlier.
Add more mayonnaise to the mixture if needed to achieve a creamy, but not goopy, consistency.
If you are adding chopped egg, gently stir it into the mixture now.
Spread butter on one side of each slice of bread, being sure to cover it completely and evenly.
Slice enough Cheddar cheese to cover two slices of bread. Set aside.
Lay one of the bread slices, butter side down, on a stovetop griddle or in a large frying pan that has been warmed on medium heat.
Cover the bread with half the slices of Cheddar cheese.
Spoon the tuna mixture on top of the cheese and spread it evenly.

Note: Depending on how large your slices of bread are, you may not use up all of your tuna mixture. Any leftover tuna would be nice on a bed of lettuce, as a salad with tomorrow night's dinner.

Arrange four pickle slices on top of the tuna mixture.
Add another layer of cheese on top of the pickles.
Top with the other slice of bread, butter side up.
Grill the assembled sandwich, lifting a corner of the sandwich occasionally with a spatula to be sure it is browning underneath.
When the bread is golden brown, carefully turn the sandwich over and brown the other side.
When the sandwich is done, lift it onto a serving plate.
Garnish plate with celery sticks and your choice of side dish. My recommendation would be Crispy Seasoned French Fries.
Serve while the sandwich is still hot.

Crispy Seasoned French Fries

Ingredients
2-1/2 pounds Russet potatoes, peeled
Cold water (enough to cover potato sticks)
1 cup white all-purpose flour
1 teaspoon garlic salt
1 teaspoon onion salt
1 teaspoon table salt
1 teaspoon paprika
1/2 cup room temperature water
1 cup vegetable oil

Instructions
Slice potatoes into long sticks, then place them in a bowl filled with cold water, so they won't turn brown while you prepare the oil.
Heat oil in a large skillet over medium-high heat.
While the oil is heating, sift the flour, garlic salt, onion salt, table salt, and paprika into a large bowl.
Gradually stir the room temperature water into the flour and salt mixture to create a creamy batter.
Dip potato sticks into the batter one at a time, then carefully place them into the hot oil. Avoid letting them touch each other at first to prevent them from sticking together.
Fry until golden brown and crispy.
Remove with tongs or slotted spoon and drain on paper towels.

Note: For a heartier version, leave the potato skins on.

Couldn't Be Easier No-Cook Ketchup

This recipe is so simple—the hardest part is making sure you have all the ingredients at hand.

If you have children, why not let them make their own ketchup? They will learn more about what's in their food, and will gain valuable hands-on food preparation experience.

Tsk tsk, and here you thought ketchup wasn't good for you.

Ingredients

12 ounces tomato paste
1/2 cup dark brown sugar, packed
1/2 teaspoon dry ground mustard
1/2 teaspoon kosher salt
1/2 scant teaspoon cinnamon
1/4 teaspoon ground cloves
1/2 teaspoon allspice
1/4 teaspoon cayenne pepper
2/3 cup water
4 tablespoons white vinegar

Instructions

With a wooden spoon, combine all ingredients in a large mixing bowl.
Stir until all the sugar is dissolved and all ingredients are well-blended.
Ladle the ketchup into an airtight container.
Refrigerate ketchup overnight to let the flavors blend.

Ketchup will last a month if kept refrigerated when not in use.

Makes 2 cups.

Miss Ancroft's Cheese and Pickle Sandwich

At noon she would take a half hour lunch break at her work station. Lunch was usually a cheese and sweet pickle sandwich, wrapped in waxed paper. That was her favorite. ~ From *Down The Tubes*

English folk are fond of cheese and pickle sandwiches, made of sharp Cheddar and Branston pickle, which is actually more of a chutney. Many Americans prefer sweet pickle chips and Velveeta on white bread, with mayonnaise.

Miss Theodesia Ancroft has her own preference for a working lunch at Citywide Post. She grew up with this version of the classic cheese and pickle sandwich and never stopped loving it. This recipe is how Miss Ancroft's mother made them for her little "Thodie".

Ingredients
2 slices hearty brown bread
4 tablespoons (half a stick) of butter, room temperature
A small brick of sharp, slightly crumbly, yellow Cheddar cheese, cut into 1/4 inch slices
Bread and Butter pickles
1/4 cup thinly sliced sweet onion, as thin as you can possibly manage. Ideally, you should have a handful of light, flaky wisps of onion.

Instructions
Generously butter one side of each slice of bread.
Scatter sliced onions over the buttered side of both slices of bread.
Working with one slice of bread, add a layer of cheese, then a layer of pickles, then another layer of cheese.
Top with the other slice of buttered and onioned bread.
Cut the sandwich from corner to corner twice, making four triangles.

Bread and Butter Pickles

Ingredients
5-1/2 cups pickling cucumbers. Look for thin skinned cucumbers.
1-1/2 tablespoons pickling, kosher or sea salt. Do not use table salt as it
has anti-clumping ingredients that are fine for the table, but not so good
for pickling.
1 cup sliced onion
1 cup white granulated sugar
1 cup white vinegar
1/2 cup apple cider vinegar
1/4 cup light brown sugar, packed
1-1/2 teaspoons mustard seed
1/2 teaspoon celery seed
1/8 teaspoon turmeric

Instructions
Thinly slice the cucumbers. Do not peel.
In a large bowl, gently stir together the cucumber slices and salt.
Cover bowl and place in the refrigerator for 2 hours.
Drain the cucumber slices in a colander.
Run cold water over them to rinse off the salt, and let them drain again.
Place the cucumber slices and onions in a large bowl.
In a medium saucepan, combine all the remaining ingredients.
Simmer on medium heat until all the sugar has dissolved.
Pour this mixture over the cucumber slices and onions.
Let the bowl sit on the counter for an hour to cool.
Cover the bowl and refrigerate for 24 hours.
Transfer pickle mixture to a large glass jar and store in refrigerator.

Pickles will keep for up to two weeks.

A Rational Engineer's Fresh and Logical Tomato Soup

Tuesday morning found Hanna Vanbrugh cooking. She didn't often make a fuss about her food, but was capable of creating a nice meal when she chose to. *It's just another form of inventing*, she thought, *taking raw materials and putting them together in ways that work.*

Hannah had never made cream of tomato soup before. *How hard can it be?* she thought, bemused as she reached for a wire basket filled with ripe tomatoes. *You take the exterior protective coating off, you break the round item down into easier to manage pieces, you heat them to change the consistency, you press the results through a sieve to remove unwanted scrap, then simmer the processed tomatoes with rich cream until warm enough to please the palate. Not nearly as difficult as building an engine, and I can certainly do that.* ~ From *Down The Tubes*

Lunch at the Lock and Key Pub

"Jack, bring us a couple of mugs of your hot cocoa with mint and some of those meat and cheese pies." Nathaniel swiveled towards me and added, sagely, "Those airships are none too warm, and ye'll appreciate havin' a hot meal in yer belly once ye get up there." ~ From *The Flight To Brassbright*

Hearty Meat Pies

Ingredients for the Filling
1 pound beef stew meat, cut into 1/2 inch pieces
Kosher salt
Cracked black pepper
2 tablespoons vegetable oil
2 tablespoons butter, room temperature
1 medium onion, finely chopped (about 1 cup)
2 sprigs of thyme with the leaves removed
2 medium Russet potatoes, cut into 1/4 inch pieces (about 3 cups)
1/4 cup dark stout beer
1/2 pound Stilton cheese
1 egg, beaten

Instructions for the Filling
Place the stew meat in a dish and season it with salt and pepper to taste.
Heat vegetable oil on medium heat in a skillet until the oil is hot, then add the stew meat.
Do not stir the meat in the pan. With a spatula, occasionally check to see if the meat has browned underneath.
When well-browned, turn each piece of meat with a fork or tongs and brown again.
Keep browning and turning until all sides of each piece of beef are browned. (Continued)

(Hearty Meat Pies Continued)

Move the beef pieces from the pan to a large bowl, and set aside.
Don't clean the pan—you will continue to use it. Just turn the heat down
to medium low.
Add the butter to the pan and let it melt.
Add the chopped onions and thyme to the pan.
Cook about 10 minutes, until the onions are soft. Stir often as they cook,
and loosen any browned pieces.
Add the diced potatoes to the pan.
Pour the stout beer over the potatoes.
Cover the pan with a well-fitting lid.
Let the pan simmer about 10 minutes, or until the potatoes become soft.
When done, scoop the contents of the pan into the bowl of cooked meat.
Scrape up any bits stuck to the pan and put them in the bowl as well.
Let the bowl of meat and potatoes cool.
When cooled to room temperature, crumble the Stilton cheese into the
meat and potatoes, and blend gently.
Taste the meat and potato filling, and add more salt and pepper if desired.

Ingredients for the Pastry
3 cups white all-purpose flour
12 tablespoons (1-1/2 sticks) very cold butter
1-1/2 teaspoons salt
6 tablespoons cold water

Instructions for the Pastry
Cut the cold butter into small pieces.
In a large bowl, stir together the flour, butter, and salt until just mixed.
Add one tablespoon of cold water, mix gently, and repeat, adding water
until the dough forms a ball.
Using light pressure, knead the dough gently on a smooth, lightly floured
surface. The warmth of your hand will finish blending the butter into the
dough.
Gather up the dough into a ball and coat it with a dusting of flour.
Wrap the dough in waxed paper or place it in a covered plastic container,
and refrigerate it for a half hour. (Continued)

Instructions for Assembling and Cooking the Meat Pies

Preheat oven to 400 degrees Fahrenheit.

On a smooth, lightly floured surface, roll out your chilled dough to 1/4 inch thick.

Cut out 4 inch round circles, using a sharp knife, large cookie cutter, or a 4 inch round dough cutter.

Cut out as many circles as you can and set them aside on a clean surface. Take all of your dough scraps and re-combine them into a ball, roll it out again to 1/4 inch thick, and cut out more circles. The goal is to make a total of 8 circles of dough.

Divide the meat and potato filling into 4 equal portions.

Working with 4 circles of dough, place one portion of filling onto each of them. Keep the filling back from the outer 1/2 inch of dough.

Brush the clean outer edge of the dough with the beaten egg.

Take the other 4 circles of dough and brush the outer 1/2 inch of one side of each with the beaten egg.

Lay one circle of dough over each filled circle of dough, with the egged edges touching. The egg acts as a glue to help hold the two halves together.

Working around the edge, pinch or fold (whichever works best for you) the two edges of dough together to create a filled and sealed pie.

Cover a rimmed baking sheet with foil.

Using a large spatula, carefully lift the pies onto the baking sheet.

Brush the top of each pie with the rest of the beaten egg.

With a sharp knife, poke several air vents in the top of each pie, to release steam.

Place the baking sheet with the pies into your oven, on a rack set to the middle position.

Bake until the pies are golden brown, about 20 minutes.

Let pies cool for 5 minutes before serving.

Rosy Red Savory Potatoes

I studied the dish set in front of me. Snugged up to the meat pie was a small mountain of savory fried potatoes. The aroma wafting up to my nose was incredibly mouthwatering. ~ From *The Flight To Brassbright*

Ingredients
6 medium red potatoes, cleaned but not peeled
1/4 cup olive oil
2 tablespoons dried rosemary leaves (the 'needles')
Salt and pepper

Instructions
Dice the potatoes into 1 inch squares.
Warm the olive oil in a large skillet over medium heat.
Add the diced potatoes to the skillet.
Place the rosemary leaves, which will resemble pine needles, in the palm of your hand. Rub your hands together over the skillet to break up the leaves and let them fall down over the potatoes.
Pause to enjoy the fragrance rising from the palms of your hands.
Add salt and pepper to taste.
Fry potatoes on medium heat until browned on the outside and fork-tender on the inside. Stir often to encourage all cut sides to brown.

Rosemary is thought to be a memory booster, so 'remember' to use it often.

Hot Cocoa with Mint

"Be right back with your drinks!" Jack promised as he trotted off again. He quickly returned with rich, warm cocoa, spiked with just enough mint to be refreshing.
~ From *The Flight To Brassbright*

Ingredients
4 cups milk
6 sprigs fresh mint
10 ounces semi-sweet or milk chocolate, broken into small pieces

Instructions
In a medium saucepan, heat the milk and mint sprigs over medium-low heat until very hot, but not boiling.
Remove the pan from the heat and let it sit for about 5 minutes.
Strain the milk through a sieve into a medium bowl, to remove the mint.
Return the milk to the saucepan and put it back on the burner, again at medium-low heat.
Gently drop the chocolate pieces into the milk.
Stir continuously with a wire whisk until the chocolate has melted and blended in, and the milk has formed a light froth.

Enjoy right away—this drink does not store well. Besides, I've never found having excess hot cocoa to be a problem, have you?

Carnival-Style Giant Turkey Legs

For a handheld portable dinner be sure to try the giant fried turkey legs! Bigger than an urchin and thrice as delicious! Napkins cost only a pewterbit extra!
~ From *The Flight To Brassbright*

In an effort to give you a healthier recipe than was served at Winthrop & Hammerschlinger's Travelling Emporium of Amazement, these turkey legs are baked. That way, you can squander those saved calories on dessert!

Ingredients

Four normal turkey legs—or two **giant** turkey legs
1/2 cup white all-purpose flour
1 teaspoon salt
1/4 teaspoon pepper
1 teaspoon Hungarian paprika
1/4 cup oil, or an oil cooking spray

Instructions

Preheat oven to 425 degrees Fahrenheit.
Mix the flour, salt, pepper, and paprika.
Pat the dry mixture onto all surfaces of the turkey legs.
Oil a baking pan large enough to hold the turkey legs.
Place the turkey legs in the baking pan, and bake for 30 minutes.
Gently turn the legs with a pair of cooking tongs, and bake for another 30 minutes.
Let the turkey legs rest for at least 10 minutes to settle their juices before serving. And really, they've been through quite a lot, so it's only polite to let them have a moment. (Continued)

(Giant Turkey Legs Continued)

Extra Advice

If possible, find some paper cone cups, such as are used for snow cones or vintage-style water coolers. Thrust the bony end of a turkey leg into a paper cone cup. Now give the cone a gentle twist to secure it around the leg. This will serve as a drip-catcher, and gives your guests a clean handle to grip as they stroll the fairgrounds, or your garden party.

Here is some good advice from Magda, a friend and foodie. "While Renaissance re-enactors (AKA BessPunks) like to integrate turkey legs into their historical roleplay, you are under no obligation to dress as Henry VIII before consuming this fowl."

Big Top Hot Roasted Peanuts

I thought about the smell of fresh hay thrown down in the elephant pen, the deep rich sound of a tiger's roar slipping in between the notions of my dreams in the deep of night, the smell of roasted peanuts on the breeze, the delighted laughter of a child genuinely enchanted by all the magic we'd contrived.
~ From *The Flight To Brassbright*

Ingredients
1 pound raw Virginia or Valencia peanuts, in their shells
1 tablespoon peanut oil
1 tablespoon kosher salt

Instructions
Preheat the oven to 350 degrees Fahrenheit.
Rinse the peanuts under cool water to remove any dirt.
Do not remove the shells!
Pat peanuts with paper towels until dry.
Place peanuts in a large bowl.
Toss with peanut oil and salt until well coated.
Spread the peanuts out in a single layer on two cookie sheets.
Roast in the oven for 10 minutes.
Shake the pans and rotate them in the oven.
Roast another 10-15 minutes.
Remove the peanuts from the oven.
Set the trays on a heatproof surface, such as a cutting board, and let the peanuts cool down.
Peanuts will continue to cook while cooling.

For best flavor, enjoy while still slightly warm.

Late Night Grab As You Can Circus Supper

Supper was a simple, late meal, usually cold cuts and cheese sandwiches heaped up on platters on the wagon counter. As the patrons left the grounds for the night, the circus folk would stop by as soon as their chores were finished and grab a sandwich or three. ~ From *The Flight To Brassbright*

Cold Cuts and Cheese Sandwiches

The circus folk traveling with Winthrop and Hammerschlinger's Travelling Emporium of Amazement are served a variety of sandwiches, depending on what is available as they roam the countryside.

Sometimes the big top is pitched near a large town, other times they perform in the heart of the farmlands. It's always a treat when fresh lettuce or tomatoes (or 'fancies' as they call these extras) are available to perk up their sandwiches.

Industralian Bubblecheese is another favorite sandwich filler. You might know of a similar cheese in your country, called "Swiss". If there's any bacon left over from breakfast, it goes in the sandwiches, too.

Cookie always makes sure there's plenty of bread. His wagon is equipped with an oven that seems to be constantly producing fresh, fragrant loaves.

Spicy mustard is always on hand, as well as fresh mayonnaise. Good condiments are a quick way to turn a humble sandwich into a delicious meal.

Cookie's "Fresh Every Day" mayonnaise recipe uses the whole egg, not just the yolk as most recipes do. He doesn't want to be bothered trying to figure out something to do with all those egg whites, and he really hates to waste food.

I Am The Very Model Of
A Condimental Mustard Soldier

Ingredients
1/2 cup apple cider vinegar
1/4 cup yellow mustard seeds
1/4 cup brown mustard seeds
1/4 cup brown ale
2 teaspoons light brown sugar, packed
3/4 teaspoon kosher salt

Instructions
Combine vinegar, mustard seeds, and beer in a medium bowl.
Cover the bowl with plastic wrap and let stand at room temperature overnight, or at least 10 hours.
Add sugar and salt to the mixture.
Pour the mixture into a blender and process until it is smooth.
Put the mustard in an airtight container. Leave out at room temperature overnight to allow the flavors to blend and mature before using.
Refrigerate after using.

Cookie's No-Waste Whole Egg
Fresh Every Day Mayonnaise

Ingredients
1/2 teaspoon dry mustard
1/4 teaspoon salt
2 eggs
2 tablespoons white vinegar
2 cups vegetable oil

Instructions
In a food processor or blender, combine mustard, salt, eggs, and vinegar.
Set your machine on medium speed and gradually drizzle in the oil while it is running. Blend until smooth and creamy.
Mayonnaise will keep for about a week, if kept refrigerated.

Un-Sunday Dinner at the Bonnet House

Ethyl propped her hands on her hips and pretended to look shocked. "Oh, heavens no, Captain! You've got to arrive on Sunday for chicken dinner, of course. Tonight we shall enjoy one of Cook's specialties—Sausage Surprise!"

Lewis groaned, and held out his upturned palm to the captain. "I've never been this unhappy to win a bet. I think the last time I had one of Cook's 'surprise' dinners, it took me a week to recover."

Ash burst out laughing. "Lewis, your stomach is more delicate than fairy wings, I swear. That sausage was delicious! I'll have yours tonight and spare you the discomfort."

Ethyl glowered. "I'll have you know that Cook completed her courses at the Primrose Kitchen Sciences Academy of Port Rivet with distinction. Thanks to her, the Bonnet House offers only the finest of cuisine." She crossed her arms and scowled good-naturedly at the men. "Now come eat, while your food's still hot."

Dinner was delightful. I ate my fill of Sausage Surprise—the 'surprise' apparently being that it was absolutely delicious. Fat buttered noodles and tiny peas in cream sauce nestled next to a very plump, succulent sausage. While I was delighted with the meal, my old nemesis the corset groaned in protest. How on earth did Ethyl keep such a svelte figure while enjoying Cook's rich, culinary creations?
~ From *The Flight To Brassbright*

Lewis's Lament
Cook's Sausage Surprise

Ingredients
6 to 8 large Bratwurst or Polish sausage links
4 green peppers
1 sweet onion, such as Vidalia
12 ounces tomato paste
15 ounces tomato sauce
1 cup water
1 tablespoon white granulated sugar
4 cloves garlic, minced
2 teaspoons basil
1 teaspoon oregano
1 teaspoon salt

Note: The basil and oregano can be either freshly chopped, or dried.

Instructions
Set a slow cooker on low.
Place sausages in the slow cooker.
Slice the green peppers and the onion.
Pile sliced peppers and onion on top of the sausages.
Spread out the pepper and onion slices to cover the sausages evenly.
In a mixing bowl, thoroughly blend the tomato paste, tomato sauce, water, sugar, garlic, basil, oregano, and salt.
Pour mixture gently into the slow cooker, taking care not to push the peppers and onions off the top of the sausages.
Put the lid on the slow cooker and let it simmer on low for 5 hours.
If you are truly in a pinch, slow cook the sausages for 2-3 hours on the high setting, but keep an eye on them to be sure nothing burns.
To serve, lift out a sausage onto a plate, then smother it with a large spoonful of the pepper and onions, as well as enough of the sauce to moisten and lend flavor.

Rich and Silky Buttered Noodles

Ingredients
16 ounces wide egg noodles
6 tablespoons butter, room temperature
Salt and pepper

Optional Ingredients
Parmesan cheese, grated
Fresh parsley, chopped

Instructions
Fill a large pot with water and bring it to a boil.
Add noodles, and let the water return to a boil.
After it boils again, turn the heat down to medium and cook noodles until they are tender—about 8-10 minutes. Carefully bite a noodle to test whether they are done.
Drain noodles in a colander.
Return drained noodles to the pot, and turn the heat under it to low.
Add the butter to the noodles, add salt and pepper to taste, and stir gently but thoroughly to coat the noodles completely.
If you wish to be fancy, arrange a serving of noodles on a plate, then sprinkle with a bit of grated parmesan cheese and freshly chopped parsley. Best served while hot.

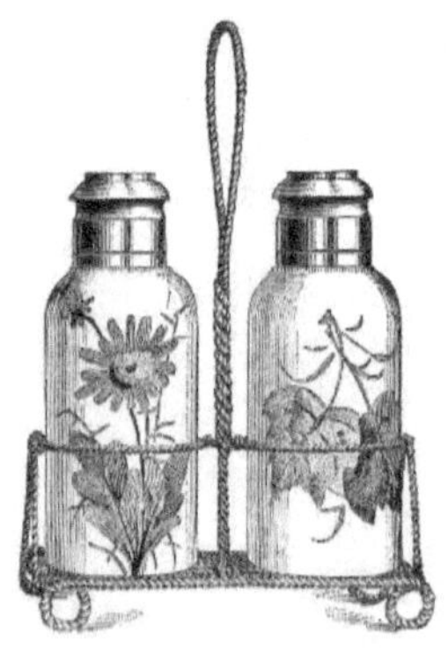

Green Peas Swimming in Cream Sauce

Ingredients

4 tablespoons butter, room temperature
4 tablespoons white all-purpose flour
2 cups whole milk
1 teaspoon salt
Pepper
1 teaspoon white granulated sugar (optional)
4 cups frozen peas

Instructions

In a quart saucepan over medium heat, melt the butter.
Whisk the flour into the butter until smooth.
Gradually add the milk, whisking it into the flour mixture.
Add salt, add pepper to taste.
Add sugar if a sweeter sauce is desired.
Keep simmering the mixture, stirring frequently, until the sauce comes to a boil.
Keep the mixture boiling for 1 full minute.
Add the frozen peas, and stir them gently into the sauce.
Put the lid on the saucepan and simmer for no more than 5 minutes at medium heat.
Serve immediately.

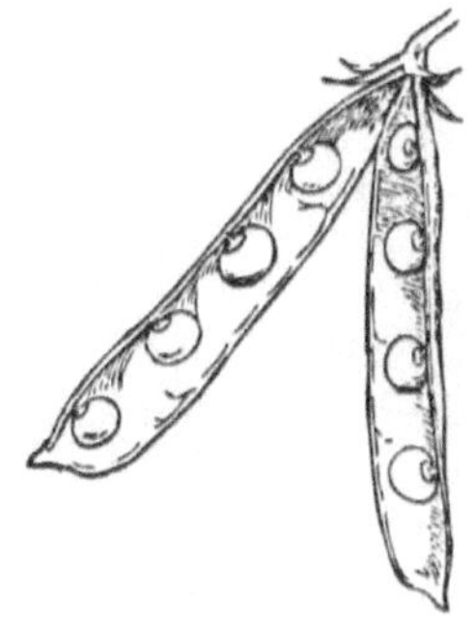

Corset's Lament
Fresh and Nutty Apple Cake

"I hope you folks saved room for apple cake!" she exclaimed.

My corset cried in earnest now, but I ignored it. "Oh, yes please, and thank you." After all, this was the last supper I could depend on. I know I'd thought that before, but this time it really was quite true. Brassbright City neither expected my arrival nor owed me any favors. ~ From *The Flight To Brassbright*

Ingredients
1/2 cup butter, room temperature
2 cups white granulated sugar
1 teaspoon vanilla
2 eggs, room temperature
2 cups white all-purpose flour
1-1/2 teaspoons baking soda
1/2 teaspoon nutmeg
1 cup walnuts, chopped fine
2 apples—peeled and cored, then shredded. Tart apples keep their flavor best in this cake.
Paper doilies
3 heaping tablespoons confectioners' sugar
2 cups whipped cream
Shortening or oil, enough to coat cake pan
White all-purpose flour, enough to coat cake pan
(Continued)

(Corset's Lament Apple Cake Continued)

Instructions

Heat oven to 325 degrees Fahrenheit.
Generously oil and flour a 9 inch Bundt pan.
In a large bowl, combine the butter, sugar, and vanilla.
Beat with an electric mixer until blended and fluffy.
Add the eggs, one by one.
Beat the mixture well after each egg.
In another bowl, mix the flour, soda, and nutmeg.
Add one cup of the flour mixture to the wet mixture, and beat for 1 minute.
Add the rest of the flour mixture and beat for another minute.
Gently fold the walnuts and apples into the batter.
Pour the batter into the prepared Bundt pan, using a spatula to scrape the bowl clean.
Slide the Bundt pan into the oven, and bake for 50 minutes.
Test the cake with a straw or skewer stuck into a wide section of the cake.
If it comes out clean, you're done. If not, bake up to 10 minutes more.
The juiciness of your apples will determine how much extra time is needed.
When done, leave the cake in the Bundt pan and set it aside to cool for 10 minutes.
Turn the Bundt pan upside down over a wire rack.
Wiggle the Bundt pan to release the cake.
Carefully turn your cake over onto a serving platter.

Instead of Frosting

Lay paper doilies over the top of the cake in a pleasing pattern.
Gently sift the confectioners' sugar over the doilies.
Carefully remove the doilies, leaving behind a sugar pattern on the cake.

Serve slices of cake with a dollop of whipped cream snugged up against the cake, so as not to disturb your sugar pattern.

Chloe's Fanciful Fish Dinner

Four hours later, Sterling left Chloe's apartment in a daze, but with a belly full of excellent broiled trout, steamed spinach, far too much chocolate, and a delicious wine he had never heard of before today. He also had an invitation to return, delivered by a breezy voice he would not soon forget. ~ From *Down The Tubes*

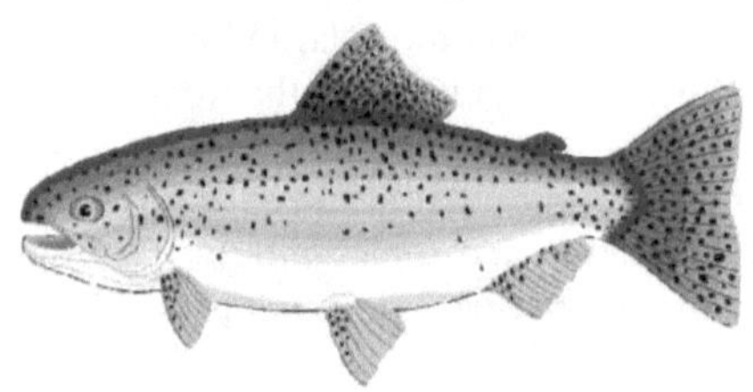

Delicately Broiled Almond Trout

Ingredients
1 pound trout, cleaned and divided into four 4-ounce servings
2 tablespoons olive oil
Sea salt
Pepper
1/4 cup slivered almonds
1 tablespoon lemon juice
1 tablespoon chopped fresh parsley

Instructions
Place trout fillets on broiler pan.
Brush trout with 1 tablespoon of the olive oil.
Sprinkle with salt and pepper to taste.
Broil 4 inches away from heat for approximately 5-10 minutes.
In a small saucepan, heat almonds in 1 tablespoon of olive oil, just until fragrant.
Add lemon juice and parsley to the almonds, and stir gently to blend.
Pour the sauce over the fish just before serving.

Fresh and Zesty Steamed Spinach

Ingredients
2-1/2 pounds freshly washed spinach. Do not dry.
Salt and pepper
1 fresh lemon, cut into wedges

Instructions
Place the wet spinach in a large saucepan.
Cover the saucepan with a lid, and cook the spinach on high heat for approximately 3 minutes, or until the leaves wilt.
Do not let them cook past the wilting stage or the texture will be lost.
When wilted, quickly remove the spinach from the pan using tongs, and place on a serving platter.
Sprinkle with salt and pepper to taste.
Garnish the platter with wedges of lemon.

Encourage diners to squeeze lemon on their spinach instead of reaching for the butter.

Victorian Era 'Hot Dogs'
Grilled Sausages on Buns

The warm summer breeze carried the scent of the cotton candy, mingled with an irresistible aroma rising from paper bags filled with hot roasted nuts, and the spicy smell of thin grilled sausage links served with mustard in clever oblong-shaped buns. ~ From *The Flight To Brassbright*

Ingredients for the Buns
1 tablespoon white granulated sugar
2-1/4 teaspoons active dry yeast
1/4 cup water
1 cup milk
1 teaspoon vegetable oil
1 teaspoon salt
4 cups white all-purpose flour
Additional oil for coating bowl

Egg Wash for Buns
1 egg
1 tablespoon cold water
Sesame seeds (optional)

Instructions for the Buns
In a large bowl, warm the water to 110 degrees Fahrenheit, using an instant-read thermometer to verify the temperature.
Dissolve the sugar in the warm water.
Sprinkle the yeast over the sugar water, and let the mixture stand for 10 minutes, or until foamy. If it does not foam, your yeast is not active, and you will need to stop until you get some fresher yeast and can try again.
Warm the milk to 110 degrees Fahrenheit, using an instant-read thermometer to verify the temperature.
Add the milk, oil, salt, and 3 cups of the flour to the yeast mixture.
If you have an electric mixer with a dough hook, beat the mixture with the hook until blended. If not, knead the dough with clean hands until blended. (Continued)

(Grilled Sausages on Buns Continued)

Mix in the last cup of flour, 1/4 cup at a time, until the dough pulls away from the sides of the bowl.
Hand knead the dough for another 5 minutes, until smooth and elastic.
Oil the inside of a large glass bowl.
Place the dough into the oiled bowl, then turn it over and over until all surfaces are coated with oil.
Cover the dough in the bowl with a clean dishcloth, and let the dough rise until it has doubled in size. This should take about an hour.
Tip the bowl so that the dough falls onto a clean, lightly oiled surface.
Divide the dough into 9 equal pieces. A round-blade pizza cutter works well for this purpose.
Using your hands, shape each piece into a ball.
Roll each ball into a cylinder 4-5 inches in length, then press down to slightly flatten them into a classic hot dog bun shape.
Place each bun on a parchment-lined baking sheet so that they are just barely touching.
Cover the sheet of buns with a clean dishcloth, and let the buns rise until they have almost doubled in size. This should take 30-45 minutes.
Preheat oven to 400 degrees Fahrenheit.
Beat the egg with 1 tablespoon of water to make an egg wash.
When your buns have risen, brush the tops of them with the egg wash.
If you like sesame seeds, sprinkle them over the egg wash.
Bake the buns for about 20 minutes, or until they are golden brown.
Move the buns to a wire rack and let them completely cool.
With a knife, split each bun lengthwise, but do not cut completely through.

Equipment Preparation for the Sausages

This recipe will require the use of a stove, as well as a gas or charcoal outdoor grill. You may wish to start your grill ahead of time, so that it is ready to use as soon as your sausages have been prepared.

Ingredients for the Sausages

9 bratwurst sausages
8-10 cups of beer. If you have a high quality beer on hand, save it for drinking. Use an inexpensive beer for this recipe.
1 large sweet onion (Vidalia is preferable)
Spicy mustard, for use when serving (Continued)

(Grilled Sausages on Buns Continued)

Instructions for the Sausages
Peel and slice the onion.
Pour the beer into a large pot, and bring it to a rolling boil.
Add the sausages and onions to the beer, and let simmer for 15 minutes.
Remove the pot from the heat and place a cover on it.
Carefully carry the covered pot outdoors and set it within reaching
distance of your grill.
Your grill should be at a medium heat; adjust as necessary.
Using tongs, lift the sausages from the beer and place them on the grill.
Cook until the bottom of each sausage has browned, then turn the
sausages and cook them until the other side browns.
Using a slotted spoon, pull the onions from the beer sauce and place in a
serving bowl.

To Serve Grilled Sausages on Buns
Place a grilled sausage in one of the split buns.
As desired, top the sausage with the beer-cooked onions and spicy
mustard.

Note: Warming your buns is optional, but it will improve the flavor of
this fun meal. Either wrap them in aluminum foil and put them on top of
your grill, or briefly lay them open-faced on the grill, to give them a toasty
texture.

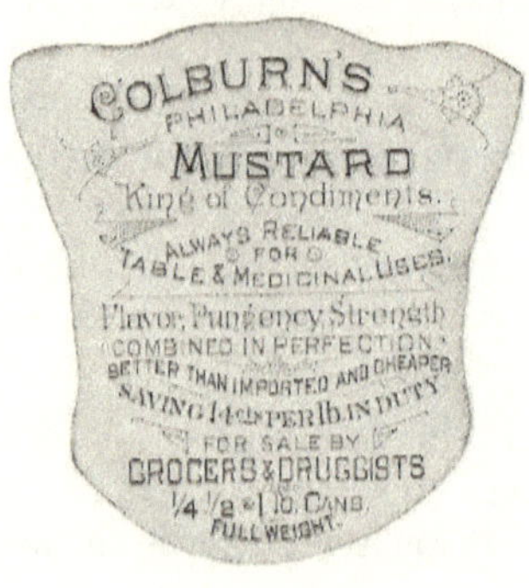

Easy Peasy Threesy Cheesy
Dinner Soufflé

And however many eggs you were thinking of buying, double it. I think I would like to make a soufflé for dinner tomorrow." ~ From *The Legend of The Engineer*

Equipment
A medium soufflé dish. A medium dish holds 22 ounces, and should measure 6 inches across and 2-1/2 inches tall.

Ingredients
7 large eggs
4 ounces sour cream
1/3 cup whole milk
Fresh ground black pepper
1 teaspoon dry mustard
1/4 teaspoon ground nutmeg
1/4 teaspoon Tabasco sauce
1 tablespoon butter, room temperature
1 ounce grated Parmesan cheese
1 ounce grated double Gloucester cheese
1 ounce grated Gruyere cheese

Instructions
Preheat oven to 350 degrees Fahrenheit.
In a large bowl, use an electric mixer to blend the eggs, sour cream, and milk for 30 seconds.
Add the black pepper, dry mustard, nutmeg, and Tabasco sauce to the egg mixture, and mix briefly to blend.
With a paper towel, coat the entire inside of the soufflé dish with butter.
Layer all the cheeses on the bottom of the soufflé dish.
(Continued)

(Easy Peasy Threesy Cheesy Dinner Soufflé Continued)

Pour the egg mixture slowly over the cheese, trying to not disturb the
arrangement of the cheese. Do not fill the soufflé dish to the top just yet.
Place the soufflé dish on a rack in the center of the hot oven.
Using a large serving spoon, carefully add more of the egg mixture to fill
the dish to the brim.
Bake for 55-60 minutes.
The soufflé is done when it is puffy and golden brown, and has risen
above the top of the dish.
Immediately present the dish to your dinner guests at the table, as the
soufflé will start to fall very quickly.

A medium size soufflé serves four very impressed dinner guests.

Coal Cookies

Letitica plucked the top recipe off her stack of cards and studied it. In truth, she could bake Coal Cookies from memory, and probably with one hand tied behind her back as well. But this was part of her tradition. She enjoyed the pondering, the planning, and the making of the shopping list.

"Right. Get three enormous sugar shacks, all the treats will need some. I know you already wrote down cocoa, but see if you can find some of those new chocolates I keep hearing about through the grapelines. They look like little mountains with a curlicue on top. I think it would be fun to add them to the Coal Cookies. Lumps inside lumps!" Letitica giggled. ~ From *The Legend of The Engineer*

Ingredients
1 cup butter, room temperature
2/3 cup white granulated sugar
1 teaspoon almond extract
1-3/4 cups white all-purpose flour
1/4 cup unsweetened cocoa powder
3/4 cup chopped nuts (pecans, almonds, or peanuts)
1/2 cup dark brown sugar, packed
1 bag (9 ounces) milk chocolate kisses

Instructions
In a medium bowl, cream together the butter and sugar. Using the back of a spoon works well for the creaming process.
Stir in the almond extract.
In another medium bowl, stir together the flour and cocoa.
Slowly add the flour mixture to the creamed butter and sugar mixture.
Mix the dough until well-blended.
Stir the nuts into the dough.
Cover the bowl of dough with plastic wrap and refrigerate for an hour.
(Continued)

(Coal Cookies Continued)

Preheat oven to 375 degrees Fahrenheit.
Unwrap the chocolate kisses.
Wrap about 1 tablespoon of dough around each chocolate kiss, forming a ball shape. The ball does not have to be perfect, as these cookies are intended to resemble lumps of coal.
Roll dough balls gently in brown sugar.
Place the dough balls 2 inches apart on an ungreased cookie sheet.
Bake for 10-12 minutes, or until no longer sticky.
With a thin metal spatula, move the cookies to a wire cooling rack.
Let the cookies cool completely.

New Year's Spicy Barrel Cake

Ingredients

2 tablespoons butter, room temperature
1-1/2 cups white all-purpose flour
3/4 teaspoon baking soda
1/4 teaspoon salt
2 teaspoons cinnamon
1/2 cup butter, room temperature
1-1/4 cups white granulated sugar
3 large eggs
1/2 teaspoon vanilla
2/3 cup whole milk

Instructions

Preheat oven to 350 degrees Fahrenheit.
Butter the interior of two round 9 inch cake pans.
Cut circles out of parchment paper to line the bottoms of the cake pans.
You can trace around the pans, and then cut slightly inside that line to make your parchment paper circles.
In a medium bowl, stir together flour, baking soda, salt, and cinnamon.
In a large bowl, cream together the butter and sugar until fully blended and creamy.
Add the eggs to the creamed butter and sugar, and beat the mixture until it is well-blended.
Blend in the vanilla.
Blend in one cup of the flour mixture.
Blend in the milk.
Blend in the rest of the flour mixture.
Do not over mix. Blend just until the dry ingredients are incorporated.
(Continued)

(Spicy Barrel Cake Continued)

Pour the batter into the cake pans, dividing it evenly between the pans.
Bake cakes for approximately 18 minutes, or until an inserted toothpick
comes out clean.
Turn the cakes out onto wire racks, parchment paper side up.
Peel off the parchment paper.
Let cakes cool completely.

Spicy Holiday Frosting

Ingredients
1/2 cup cream cheese, room temperature (half of an 8-ounce package)
1/2 cup butter, room temperature
2 tablespoons whole milk
1-1/2 teaspoons cinnamon
2-1/2 cups confectioners' sugar

Instructions
In a large bowl, use an electric mixer set on low speed to blend the cream
cheese and butter.
Blend the milk and cinnamon into the cream cheese and butter mixture.
Add 1 cup of confectioners' sugar, and beat on medium speed until
creamy.
Add additional confectioners' sugar, beating after each addition, until
frosting reaches a good consistency for spreading.
If the frosting becomes too stiff, add an additional teaspoon of milk at a
time to bring it back to a spreadable consistency.

Frosting the Cake
Place one cake on a decorative serving platter.
Frost the top of the cake.
Add the second cake on top of the frosted layer.
Frost the top and the sides, completely covering the cake.

Not So Sweet Cake

He bid me good day, but never once looked me in the eye. He brought me more food, including two pieces of cake. Where would he have found cake? It seemed like guilt-cake to me, and didn't taste very sweet. ~ From *The Flight To Brassbright*

Ingredients

2 cups white granulated sugar
1-3/4 cups white all-purpose flour
3/4 cup unsweetened cocoa powder
1-1/2 teaspoons baking powder
1-1/2 teaspoons baking soda
1 teaspoon salt
2 eggs
1 cup low fat milk
1/2 cup vegetable oil
1 teaspoon vanilla
1 cup boiling water
Shortening or oil, enough to coat cake pan
White all-purpose flour, enough to coat cake pan

Instructions

Preheat oven to 350 degrees Fahrenheit.
Oil and flour a 9 inch x 13 inch sheet cake pan.
In a large bowl, stir together the sugar, flour, cocoa, baking powder, baking soda, and salt.
Add the eggs, milk, oil, and vanilla, and blend the mixture for 2 minutes with an electric mixer on medium speed.
Stir in the boiling water. Batter will be thin.
Pour batter evenly into the prepared pan.
Bake 35 minutes, or until an inserted toothpick comes out clean.
Let cake cool in the pan for 10 minutes.
Turn cake onto a wire rack to finish cooling completely.
Serve as is, unfrosted.

(Editor's Note: This recipe *obviously* needs more frosting!)

Letitica's Luscious Late Night Chocolate Cake

"After I finished my story, we shared a late dinner. While savoring a thick slice of chocolate cake for dessert, I coaxed my new friend into telling me more about herself." ~ From *The Flight To Brassbright*

Dry Ingredients
1-3/4 cups white all-purpose flour
3/4 cup unsweetened cocoa powder
1-1/2 teaspoons baking powder
1-1/2 teaspoons baking soda
2 cups white granulated sugar
1 teaspoon salt

Wet Ingredients
2 large eggs
1/2 cup vegetable oil
1 cup whole milk
2 teaspoons vanilla
1 cup boiling water

Note: If you are able to use duck eggs, they are magnificent in cakes!

Instructions
Preheat oven to 350 degrees Fahrenheit.
In a large bowl, stir together all of the dry ingredients.
In a small bowl, mix the wet ingredients, except the boiling water.
Slowly add the wet ingredients to the dry ingredients, mixing with a spoon as you add them.
When just blended, use an electric mixer set on low speed and beat the batter for 2 minutes. (Continued)

(Late Night Chocolate Cake Continued)

Slowly add the boiling water while still beating.
Beat for another full minute. The batter will be thin.
Pour the batter evenly into a 9 inch x 13 inch sheet cake pan.
Place the cake pan in your oven on a center rack, and bake for 35-40
minutes, or until an inserted toothpick comes out clean.

This cake is quite rich and can hold its own without frosting. But if you
simply must, use your favorite frosting recipe or top with stiffly whipped
cream and berries.

Just Desserts Chocolate Cake

Max interrupted my mental woolgathering. "I'd walk you down there miss, but I need to sweep the shop after closing, and I promised Ma I'd bring home a chocolate cake from 'Just Desserts' next door, for dinner." He scuffed the toe of his boot against the floorboards nervously as he spoke. It was adorable.
~ From *The Flight To Brassbright*

Ingredients
2 cups white granulated sugar
1-3/4 cups white all-purpose flour
3/4 cup unsweetened cocoa
1-1/2 teaspoons baking powder
1-1/2 teaspoons baking soda
1 teaspoon salt
3 eggs
1 cup milk
1/2 cup vegetable oil
2 teaspoons almond extract
1 cup boiling water
Shortening or oil, enough to coat cake pans
White all-purpose flour, enough to coat cake pans

Instructions
Preheat oven to 350 degrees Fahrenheit.
Oil and flour two 9 inch round cake pans.
In a medium bowl, stir together the sugar, flour, cocoa, baking powder, baking soda, and salt.
Add the eggs, milk, oil, and vanilla, then stir to blend.
Mix the batter for 3 minutes with an electric mixer on medium speed.
With a large spoon, stir the boiling water into the batter. The batter will be thin. (Continued)

(Just Desserts Chocolate Cake Continued)

Pour the batter into the greased pans, dividing the batter evenly between both pans.
Bake for 30-35 minutes, or until an inserted toothpick comes out clean.
Let the pans cool for 10 minutes.
Carefully turn the cakes out of the pans. The easiest way to do this is to invert a plate over each pan, and then turn both the plate and pan over together.
Carefully move one cake onto a serving platter.
Frost the top of the cake with chocolate buttercream frosting.
Add the second cake on top of the frosted layer.
Frost the top and sides of the cake, using a spatula to create a decorative whorled design.

Chocolate Buttercream Frosting

Ingredients
1-1/2 cups butter, room temperature
1 cup unsweetened cocoa powder
5 cups confectioners' sugar
1/2 cup whole milk
2 teaspoons vanilla
1/4 cup finely chopped toasted almonds (optional)

Instructions
Cream the butter with the back of a spoon until it is light and fluffy.
Cream the cocoa and confectioners' sugar into the butter.
Blend in the milk and vanilla.
Beat with an electric mixer on medium speed, until it is an easy to spread consistency.
After you have frosted the cake, scatter the chopped almonds over the top of the cake, if desired.

Puffy Pillow Mint Candies

Ingredients
4-1/4 to 4-1/2 cups confectioners' sugar
1/4 cup butter, room temperature
1/4 cup heavy whipping cream
1/8 teaspoon peppermint oil
Gel food coloring, use colors of your choice

Instructions
In a large bowl, place all of the ingredients, except the gel food coloring. Using an electric mixer on low speed, blend the ingredients. Then increase the mixer speed to medium, and beat until stiff.
When the dough becomes very stiff, pour it onto a surface dusted with confectioners' sugar, and knead the dough it until it is soft and smooth, but not sticky.
Using a sharp knife, cut the dough into eight equal pieces.
Put the pieces into a closed container so they don't dry out.
One piece at a time, remove the dough and add a few drops of gel food coloring.
Knead the dough until the color is spread evenly throughout.
With the palms of your hands, roll the dough into a rope about 10 inches long and 1/4 inch thick.
Using a sharp knife, cut the rope into small squares, about 1/4 inch wide.
Place the squares on a sheet of waxed paper. Cover with another sheet of waxed paper, and let the mints dry for 8-10 hours.
These mints are best eaten promptly, but can be stored in a sealed plastic container and kept refrigerated for up to one week.

Cotton Candy

"That's the *Silver Swan*. And it is most definitely first class travel, the likes of which we are never likely to experience, alas. Did you know it has a kitchen, with its own chef? I wonder what sort of food the fancy people like to eat up in the sky?"

I grinned as an image formed in my mind. "Cotton candy. That way they could gaze at the clouds while eating one!" We both had a good laugh at that.
~ From *The Flight To Brassbright*

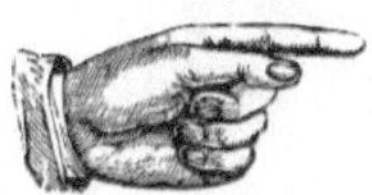 **Warning:** This recipe involves the use of **hot sugar**, which can result in personal injury or damage to plastic surfaces. Please exercise caution!

This recipe makes about twelve fluffy cotton candy balls.

Equipment and Preparation
Clean tarp or sheets of plastic
Heavy object, such as a thick cutting board or an old phone book
2 wooden spoons
Olive or vegetable oil
Goggles or other protective eyewear
Wire cutters
Large wire whisk, one you won't mind ruining
Candy thermometer
12 small serving bowls

You will need to clear a workspace on your kitchen counter, and protect it from possible hot sugar drippage. You will also want to protect the front of your counter and the floor with a tarp or sheets of plastic.
Place the heavy object near the front edge of your cleared counter space. This will be used to anchor the wooden spoons in place.
Prepare 2 wooden spoons by coating their handles with oil. Secure the oiled wooden spoons underneath the heavy object, 6-8 inches apart, with the spoon handles extending out past the front edge of the kitchen counter.
Now put on your goggles, or other protective eyewear. Use the wire cutters to snip the round ends off of the whisk wires, so that they become straight, open tines. (Continued)

(Cotton Candy Continued)

Ingredients

2-1/2 cups white granulated sugar
1/2 cup plus 2-1/2 tablespoons light corn syrup
1/2 cup plus 1 tablespoon water, room temperature
2 to 3 drops food coloring, use color of your choice

Instructions

In a heavy-bottomed medium saucepan, stir together the sugar, corn syrup, and water.
Simmer the mixture on medium-high heat, until a candy thermometer reads 320 degrees Fahrenheit.
Pour the sugar mixture into a microwave safe medium glass bowl.
Add the food coloring and stir to blend.
Place the glass bowl in your work area, near the wooden spoons.

Note: If you have a lab coat and protective gloves, don them now. You're about to perform Kitchen Science!

Dip the tines of the modified whisk into the hot sugar mixture.
Let the sugar mixture drain off of the tines for a few seconds, until it starts to form strands.
Stand in front of the wooden spoon handles, and carefully wave the whisk around the handles to create sugar strands.
The sugar strands should drift down and be caught on the spoon handles.
Keep making strands as quickly as you can work.
When you have made enough strands to create a ball, slide the strands off of the spoon handles and gently form them into a ball. Then place the ball into a small serving dish.
Keep making strands and forming cotton candy balls, placing each ball in its own serving dish.
If your sugar mixture starts to thicken, microwave it in 20 second bursts until it becomes liquid and bubbly again.

Serve the cotton candy balls promptly. Any humidity in the air will start to dissolve the sugar.

Cleanup

Let all of your cooking equipment cool completely (hot sugar can be destructive to any plastic it touches), then give it all a long soak in hot soapy water.

"Frostica Pieces" Cracked Ice Candy

"Tsk, tsk, I really should make you go round to the front door if you're going to beg for sweets, Miss Margaret," Letitica mock-scolded. "But here, I can't resist a piece myself." She picked up two shards of Crackled Ice and held one of them out the window, dangling it from her fingertips.

Margaret's hand quickly swiped it and popped it into her mouth. "Thank you Missus Liddle!" the girl mumbled around her mouthful of candy. "Frostica pieces! I love these." ~ From *The Legend of The Engineer*

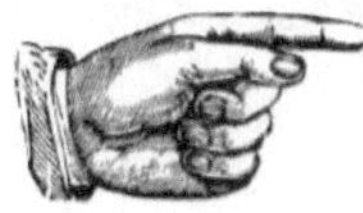

Warning: This recipe involves the use of **hot sugar**, which can result in personal injury or damage to plastic surfaces. Please exercise caution!

Equipment
Cookie sheet with raised sides
Medium saucepan
Candy thermometer
Waxed paper
Large cutting board
Small hammer

Ingredients
Oil, either bottled or spray
3-1/2 cups white granulated sugar
2 cups water, room temperature
1 cup light corn syrup
1/4 teaspoon Cream of Tartar

Instructions
Lightly oil the cookie sheet, including the raised sides. Be mindful to get the oil into the corners and creases. Set sheet aside on a flat surface. Mix the sugar, water, corn syrup, and Cream of Tartar in a medium saucepan. (Continued)

(Crackled Ice Candy Continued)

While stirring constantly, slowly bring the mixture to a boil on medium
heat. This can take a long time, but don't rush it or the mixture will burn.
As the mixture reaches a boil, it will change from cloudy to clear.
Once the temperature of the mixture reaches 300 degrees Fahrenheit
(hard crack temperature), remove it from the heat. Don't allow the
temperature to rise beyond 320 degrees Fahrenheit, or it will turn brown.
Slowly pour the mixture onto your oiled cookie sheet. A slow, steady pour
will avoid forming bubbles in your finished candy.
Let the candy harden and cool for at least an hour. It should be very hard
to the touch, once it has cooled completely.
Cover a large cutting board with a sheet of waxed paper.
Turn the pan over and let the candy fall out onto the waxed paper.
If any candy sticks to the pan, warm a thin metal spatula in hot water and
use it to loosen the stuck bits.
Cover the candy with another sheet of waxed paper.
Tap the candy lightly all over with a hammer to break it into small pieces.

This candy is best enjoyed promptly, but can be stored in a sealed plastic
container, and kept refrigerated overnight. Any longer than that, and the
candy will lose its crispness and start to become gummy.

Perkylater Coffee

"Why don't you make us some coffee and I'll tell you a story, Missus Liddle?" I offered.

"A decrepit idea! I've got some fancy coffee droppings I've been saving for a special occasion. My belated husband brought them back from a trip to Sooty Springs twenty years ago. They should be well-aged by now!"

She nodded rapidly, eager to hear more. "Just let me get the coffee brewing in the Perkylater and you can continue your story." She shuffled over to her stove and pulled an odd device from the back burner. From the top down, this 'Perkylater' featured a small copper lid, which covered a rounded glass pot, which sat atop another glass pot. Both were connected with a clever joining ring and a tube that ran up through the middle. The lower pot was half-clad in copper, which flared out at the bottom. It looked quite confusing, but was rather pretty.

"That's an interesting way to make coffee, Missus Liddle," I said.
~ From *The Flight To Brassbright*

What Is A Percolator?
The coffee percolator is one of those devices that has fallen out of fashion. Drip coffee makers, introduced in the 1970s, brew coffee at a lower heat than a percolator, and thus produce a less bitter coffee. Most percolators still in use have since been demoted to camping duty.

A percolator consists of a carafe-like pot. Inside the pot, a metal tube runs up through the center of a perforated metal basket. The pot is filled with water, and the coffee grounds are placed in the metal basket. When the water reaches a boil, it travels up through the tube, and pours out over the grounds. After draining through the grounds, it returns to the bottom of the pot. There it again reaches a boil, goes up the tube and over the grounds, and back down to the bottom to cycle again. And again. And again.

A coarse grind coffee is used in a percolator, in order to stand up to the constant 'washing' of the boiling water. A fine grind coffee will wash right through the perforated basket, resulting in muddy sludge in your cup.
(Continued)

(Perkylater Coffee Continued)

Equipment and Ingredients
Percolator
Coarse grind coffee. If possible, use a low acid coffee.
Cool or room temperature water

Instructions
Open the percolator, remove the perforated metal basket and tube
assembly, then add water. Use 8 ounces of water for each cup of coffee
you intend to brew. Make sure you don't overfill the pot; the water line
must stop below the metal basket.
Put the perforated metal basket and tube assembly back into the pot. Add
coffee to the metal basket, using two teaspoons for each cup of coffee
you intend to brew.
Depending on the type of percolator you're using, either turn it on
(electric) or place it on a stove burner set to high.
When the 'perking' slows and then stops, turn it off or remove it from the
heat. Don't allow the coffee to perk beyond 3 minutes.
The coffee is now ready to drink.

Mulled Spicy Red Wine

The kitchen clocks—all six of them—chimed, chirped and bonged out the hour of six o'clock. Letitica wiped her hands on a towel, glanced around the kitchen and smiled. Plates of treats were strewn all over the kitchen table, while a pot of spiced wine simmered gently on the stove, adding to the enticing aromas mingling in the air. ~ From *The Legend of The Engineer*

Ingredients

2 bottles of your favorite red wine
1 cup apple cider
3/4 cup light brown sugar, packed
3 cinnamon sticks
1 teaspoon vanilla
2 whole star anise
2 oranges, halved and sliced, not peeled
2 lemons, halved and sliced, not peeled

Instructions

Combine all of the ingredients in a slow cooker set on medium heat.
Put the lid on the slow cooker, and let the wine warm for an hour.
If it nears a boil during the hour, turn the heat down to low.
Using a pair of tongs, lift out the fruit slices and set them in a small bowl next to the slow cooker.
Run a small handheld strainer through the wine to remove the spices.

To serve, ladle warm wine into cups. Garnish each with a slice of the spiced fruit. Leave the slow cooker set on low until all of the wine has been served.

Note: If you do not have a slow cooker, you can use a large pot on your stovetop, but you must watch it carefully.

Orange Marmalade

As daddy used to tell me, "Friends are just strangers who haven't yet barged into your house and eaten all your favorite marmalade."
~ From *The Flight To Brassbright*

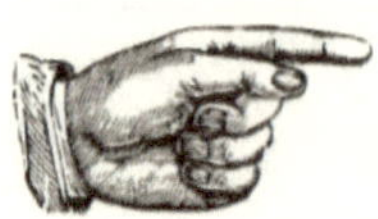 Please follow proper, safe canning techniques. If you have never canned, consider learning the art of food preservation. Look for local extension courses, or take the online education offered by Ball.

Equipment
10 8-ounce jelly jars, with rings and lids. If you intend to freeze, rather than can your jelly, use freezer-safe glass canning jars.
8-quart saucepot
Citrus zesting tool
Candy thermometer
Small glass or ceramic plate

Ingredients
4 to 5 medium oranges
1 very ripe lemon
6 cups water
7-1/2 cups white granulated sugar

Instructions
Wash the outer skin of the oranges and lemon thoroughly.
With a zesting tool, remove only the yellow portion of the lemon skin.
Do not use the bitter white pith.
With a knife, cut the lemon in half, then juice the halves.
Cut the oranges into 1/8 inch slices.
Remove the seeds from the orange slices.
Stack the orange slices and cut them into quarters.
Pause to admire your work.
Place the small glass or ceramic plate into your freezer. (Continued)

(Orange Marmalade, Continued)

Place the oranges, lemon zest, lemon juice, and water into an 8-quart
saucepot.
Set the pot on the stove, turn the heat to high, and bring the fruit and
water to a boil.
Once the fruit and water are boiling, reduce the heat to maintain an
active simmer.
Cook for about a half hour, stirring often.
When the fruit is very soft, turn the heat to high, and bring it to a full boil.
Add the sugar to the fruit mixture.
Stir constantly while bringing the mixture up to 223 degrees Fahrenheit.
Watch carefully to avoid a boil-over. At this stage, the mixture should
begin to darken.
Dip out a teaspoon of the mixture, and drop it onto the chilled plate.
After 30 seconds, tilt the plate. If the mixture has become jelly-like and
only moves a little, it is ready. If it is thin and runny, keep cooking it.
Clean and return your plate to the freezer between tests.
Re-test the mixture occasionally, until it reaches a jellied consistency.

If you plan to use the hot water bath preservation method, fill the jelly
jars with the marmalade, leaving 1/2 inch of headspace. Then follow
proper canning procedures and process the jars for 10 minutes.
If you plan to freeze the marmalade instead, leave 2 inches of headspace
in your freezer-safe glass canning jars (to allow for expansion).

Illustration is from *Science in the Kitchen* by Mrs. E. E. Kellogg, published in 1893.
It is a fascinating book, which you can read for free at Project Gutenberg.

Gooseberry Jelly

"Oh, and I should check the terminal gift shop too. I know someone in Meridian who loves gooseberry jelly."

I gave him a quizzical look. "Gooseberry jelly?"

"Sure thing, miss, some of the best there is! Ya see, it's mostly farmland beyond the town limits, and those farmers make good use of the air routes to ship out small specialty items, such as jellies and preserves, and some tasty hard cider. They also keep the gift shops here stocked with treats for the forgetful travelers who neglected to buy a present before flying off to visit relatives."
~ From *The Flight To Brassbright*

 Please follow proper, safe canning techniques. If you have never canned, consider learning the art of food preservation. Look for local extension courses, or take the online education offered by Ball.

Ingredients
4-1/2 to 5 pounds fully ripe gooseberries
1 cup water
1-3/4 ounces dry pectin
1/2 teaspoon butter, room temperature
7 cups white granulated sugar

Instructions
Place the ripe berries and water into a large saucepan.
Bring the berries to a boil, then reduce the heat to low.
Put the lid on the saucepan and simmer the berries for 10 minutes.
Remove the berries from the heat.
Drape three layers of damp cheesecloth in a large colander, then set the colander into a large bowl. This bowl will catch the juice as it drains through the cheesecloth. (Continued)

(Gooseberry Jelly Continued)

Pour the cooked berries into the cheesecloth, then lift up the edges of the cheesecloth and tie them closed to form a bag.
As the bowl begins to fill with berry juice, occasionally pour the juice off into another bowl. This will allow more juice to continue to drip through the cheesecloth bag.
Press gently on the cheesecloth bag from time to time, to encourage the juice to continue to drip.

Alternately, you can use a jelly bag and strainer stand over a bowl or tall pitcher (using a pitcher will reduce juice splashing onto the counter).

When the gooseberries have stopped dripping, collect all the juice and measure it.
For this recipe, you need exactly 5-1/2 cups of gooseberry juice. If you are a little short of juice, you may add up to 1/2 cup of water to make up the difference.
Pour the juice into a large saucepan.
Stir the pectin into the juice.
Add the butter to the juice to help prevent foaming.
Bring the juice to a full boil. You want a rolling boil that keeps going when you stir it.
Pour in all the sugar.
Stirring constantly, bring the mixture back up to a rolling boil.
Remove from heat, and skim off any foam that might have formed.

If you plan to use the hot water bath preservation method, fill the jelly jars, leaving 1/2 inch of headspace. Then follow proper canning procedures and process the jars for 10 minutes.
If you plan to freeze the jelly instead, leave 2 inches of headspace in your freezer-safe glass canning jars (to allow for expansion).

Victuals! A Salon Talk

For fun, I'm including the transcript of a salon lecture I presented in November 2011, in the virtual world of Second Life. In that world, I'm known by my avatar's name, Ceejay Writer. You'll see some references that may fly over your head, if you're not familiar with the City of New Babbage in that reality, but you are welcome to just smile, nod, and keep reading.

What's that bubbling in the pot on the stove? SCIENCE! Kitchen technology took great strides in the Victorian era, thanks in part to discoveries by Louis Pasteur, Gale Borden, George B. Simpson and many other inventive and scientific minds. Learn about surprising changes in food preparation of yesteryear—and how you can bring a bit of vintage techniques into your kitchen of today.

Salon presenter Ceejay Writer practices what she preaches. In her First Life, she grows and preserves foods to last through the winter months. She is a self-taught herbalist with extensive herb and tea gardens, an organic vegetable gardener and forest forager. Besides traditional canning, she enjoys figuring out new uses for her beloved dehydrator. Most of her favored food preparation methods pre-date her own birth.

Introduction by Baron Klaus Wulfenbach, avatar and proprietor of the Aether Salon in the steampunk City of New Babbage.

Good afternoon, gourmets, connoisseurs, foodies and people who like to eat!

Before I begin, let me preface my talk by explaining that I am a born-and-bred American, and come from a rich heritage of American pioneers. My family emigrated from Italy in 1635 (in fact the Albertis were the first Italian emigrants to set foot on American soil), and from England in the early 1700's, settling in New York/New Amsterdam, Canada, Michigan and Missouri.

As the nation began to Go West, my family hopped in covered wagons, settling in Utah and Southern California. Much of what I have learned about cooking and food preservation is based on the history and traditions passed down to me through the generations.

I'm a hybrid who loves a shiny espresso maker just as much as a bale wire canning jar. I'm lucky enough to live in the countryside and have a good amount of land. I grow a lot of our food and prepare it to take us through the winter months.

I've definitely got one foot in the past and one in the present, and I like it that way. But my upbringing means that a lot of what I know and do is decidedly American. Many of you are *not* Americans, I know!

However, I encourage you to take what you like from this talk and expand on it. Use it as a springboard to learn more about your own history and culture, and bring a bit of it to your kitchen and onto your dining table.

The Victorian Era was an amazing time to be a Foodie! Many changes in American eating habits developed as the citizens got settled in and stopped moving around so much. As home life became more stable, we demanded much more from our kitchens. We wanted better food, faster, easier, and reliable ways to store it.

One of my favorite foodies of the day was Fannie Farmer. She graduated from one of the first American cooking schools, The Boston Cooking School, and in 1896 published (at her own expense) the Boston Cooking-School Cookbook. Versions of her book are still in use today.

Thanks in great part to Fannie, our recipes became more exact. She removed the guesswork from recipes and helped standardize the American measurement system. Precise measurements came into use instead of 'pinches' and 'butter the size of an egg'. She earned the nickname "The Mother of Level Measurements". Explicit instructions were a huge boon to novice cooks, as it takes many years to develop a natural sense of 'when just enough is right.'

But, it's no good having well-prepared food if it's not safe to eat! We owe a debt of thanks to Louis Pasteur, who in 1856 figured out how to make our food much safer. His process of Pasteurization kills bacteria in milk, juice, and many other foods.

The urchins in the Salon may want to gather in closer now, cause we're about to talk about something rather gross. In 1859 Louis Pasteur entered a contest sponsored by the French Academy of Sciences. The goal was to devise an experiment that would disprove the belief in "spontaneous generation".

What, you may ask, is spontaneous generation? It was a longstanding belief that dated back to before the Middle Ages. Basically, people believed that decaying matter could suddenly produce life forms.

Here's a spontaneous regeneration recipe from the 17th century, and I swear I am not making this up! How to produce mice: Put your sweaty stinky underwear into a jar, add wheat husks and wait three weeks. During that time, the sweat would soak into the husks and turn them into mice.

Knowing all we know today, of course that was absurd thinking. Mice were sneaking in after those wheat husks, of course. But this is the sort of mindset that needed to be shattered.

Anyway, Pasteur's contest experiment had him boiling meat broth in a flask, then heating the neck of the flask enough to bend it into an S shape. The S allowed air to enter, but microorganisms settled out in the S curve, thanks to gravity.

The broth did not produce any microorganisms. However, when he tilted the flask to let the broth slide up into the S curve, where all the icky stuff had settled, THEN the broth turned cloudy and went awful.

This new information about the effects of air and microorganisms on food helped pave the way for advances in food storage techniques.
Now the notion of putting food into metal cans has been around a long time. Decades before Pasteur changed the way we thought about food safety, we had started sealing food into containers. In 1810, Peter Durand figured out how to put food into cans.

His invention went into use in the British Navy a few years later. Sounds good so far, right? Well, the cans were made of solid iron with a thin coating of tin that clearly outweighed their contents. Now, let's assume you're hungry and you'd actually like to get AT those contents.

Grab a can opener? Nope. They haven't been invented yet and won't be for a long time. The recommended method to get at your ironclad foodstuffs was to get a hammer and chisel and work your way around the top. Some people couldn't be bothered with that method and used bullets or bayonets to try to get at their supper.

Any nutritional benefits of the canned food was surely offset by the risk of injury from the method of opening, or the metal shards that might get bashed into your food and ingested... clearly, the food can was an idea needing a lot of work.

In the 1860s, steel cans replaced those old iron ones—and hurrah, they were much thinner! In fact, in 1858, Ezra Warner was the first person to obtain a patent on a can opener. Clearly, he was anticipating this great advancement in canning technology.

His can opener had a blade that could be shoved into the rim of the can and then forced around the edge. Warner was obviously a New Babbager, if only in spirit, as he claimed in his patent that "a child may use it without difficulty, or risk."

But you wouldn't find Ezra's can opener in any kitchen. When you purchased your canned goods, you'd ask the store clerk to open them for you, using the stores can opener. And then you'd take them home. Any benefit of long-term storage ended the moment you bought your food.

In 1870, William Lyman invented that handy little cutting wheel that goes around the rim of a can, and eventually the contraption settled out into something that became a must-have in every kitchen.

While tin cans are one method of long-term food storage, a more hands-on approach is home canning, which in spite of the name, uses glass jars and not cans. Home-canning techniques have changed vastly through the years, but the benefits have always been clear. Growing your own food and canning it allows you to stretch the household budget, and preserve your harvest through the winter months.

Even those who don't grow produce can benefit from taking advantage of good prices for seasonal fresh fruit and vegetables. It's also a chance to prepare extra luxuries, such as jams, jellies, relishes, and pickles. Unlike tin cans, glass jars are re-usable and the contents can be seen through the container.

I could spend hours talking about canning, as it's a topic dear to me—and I'd be happy to offer advice or instructions later to anyone wishing to learn more. But for this salon, let's just focus on one brilliant, eccentric woman who was influential in this area.

Amanda Jones was a scientist who invented the vacuum method of canning. Basically that means sucking all of the air out of a container, thus making it impossible for bacteria to grow. She got the idea from her spirit guides. Yes, you heard me right. Amanda held a strong belief in spirit guides. She said that a spirit had helped her find a key when she was eight years old. A few years later, one of her brothers died. She claims to have contacted him after his death, and from then on she valued the advice of her many spirit guides.

One day, a spirit guide described to her the vacuum canning process, and suggested that she contact a man named Cooley. She had never canned anything in her life, but she did get in touch with Cooley. In 1873, they created what would be called the "Jones Process".

Ten years later, she founded the Women's Canning and Preserving Company. At first, they only hired women to work there. But three years later, men were finally allowed to be hired. They promptly took over the company and tossed Amanda out. Too bad her spirit guides didn't warn her *that* was coming!

Now let's move on to some fun devices that help us make our food tasty. How many of you like... toast? It's one of my favorite snacks! People have been making toast for eons. It was originally a way to preserve bread once it had lost its fresh-baked texture. It's also a very handy communication device for sending us images of deities and aging rock stars, lightly burned into our bread, in hopes we will alert Ripley's or the Weekly World News.

In the Pre-Toaster Era, hunks of bread were laid on hot stones or held up to a fire. In fact, the word 'toast' is derived from the Latin 'tostum' which means to scorch or burn.

In England in the 1870s, the first toasters began to appear. These were simple iron heating coils that a slice of bread could be leaned against. The bread needed to be hand-turned to get both sides toasted. Still, it was pretty techie compared to hot rocks. But these first machines were slightly inconvenient, as they had a tendency to rust, melt, and start fires.

In later years, General Electric pioneered the use of nickel and chromium in the coils, which eliminated that tendency to melt. The toaster has undergone constant refining and improvement ever since—proof that we all are seeking the Perfect Slice of Toast. Someday, I predict that we shall even have Talking Toasters!

Now then. Is Saffia Widdershins in the room? Because we are going to talk about technology beneficial to CAKE. A light fluffy cake often requires well-beaten eggs. And there was a time when eggbeaters as we know them did not exist!

Cooks would instead use a "broad-bladed knife" or "clean switches, peeled and dried" to whip those egg whites into meringue, and that was very fatiguing work!

Enter intrepid inventor Rufus M. Eastman, who in 1885 created a mixer which could be powered by hand, by electricity, or even by water. Pretty fun notion, but it didn't catch on.

The man history remembers is Willie Johnston, who one year earlier had devised a beater that used a wheel and well-placed gears to spin the beater blades. His machine was dual-action as well. It would mix eggs in one bowl and dry ingredients in another, both at the same time! Bet that was fun to watch.

So we've touched upon inventions that produce toast, and cake—two favored treats in the Steamlands. But I would be remiss if I did not acknowledge the device that makes that irresistible, beloved food… Waffles!

All hail Cornelius Swartwout of Troy, New York! On August 24th, 1869, he became the first inventor to patent a waffle maker. His device was clever and practical, making good use of the stoves of the time.

The Swartwout Waffle Maker was designed to fit exactly into one of those round openings on a woodstove. You'd pull out the stove lid, insert the waffle iron ring, and then set the waffle iron into the ring.

To cook a waffle, you'd open up the waffle iron, add your batter, close it, and then let the waffle cook. After a short time, you'd flip the waffle iron in the ring to brown the other side of your waffle.

Atop that waffle, you could then heap fruit preserves, thanks to canning techniques, and whipped cream, courtesy of the eggbeater. Serve that up with a big glass of pasteurized milk, thanks to our friend Mr. Pasteur. Life in the Victorian era could be both safe and delicious.

By the way, National Waffle Day is celebrated on August 24th in the United States, in honor of Cornelius Swartwout's wonderful invention.

About the Author

Lori Alden Holuta lives between the cornfields of mid-Michigan, where she grows vegetables and herbs, when she's not playing games with a cat named Chives. She's fond of activities from the past, including canning and preserving, crocheting, and cooking.

Her lifelong fascination with the Victorian era dovetailed nicely with articles she wrote for *The Primgraph*, a magazine which focused on historical eras in virtual worlds, as well as music and book reviews for *Steampunk Magazine*.

Books by Lori Alden Holuta

The Brassbright Chronicles

The Flight to Brassbright

Brassbright Kids

Full Steam Ahead
A Short Story Collection Where Kids Save the Day

Brassbright Cooks

Steamed and Steamy
Recipes from the Steampunk World of Industralia

Shredding It
A Cabbage Cookbook

Where To Find Lori's Books

brassbrightcity.com

books2read.com/LoriAldenHoluta

Connect with Lori Alden Holuta

I really appreciate your interest in my cookbook! Here's how to find me in the aethernet.

The Brassbright Chronicle
brassbrightcity.com

A License to Quill
ceejaywriter.com

X
x.com/LoriAldenHoluta

Facebook
facebook.com/brassbright

Pinterest
pinterest.com/holuta

Recipe Index

www.ingramcontent.com/pod-product-compliance
Lightning Source LLC
Chambersburg PA
CBHW031442130726
47989CB00003B/1252